Red Jack

Mary Durack

illustrated by Michael Wilkin

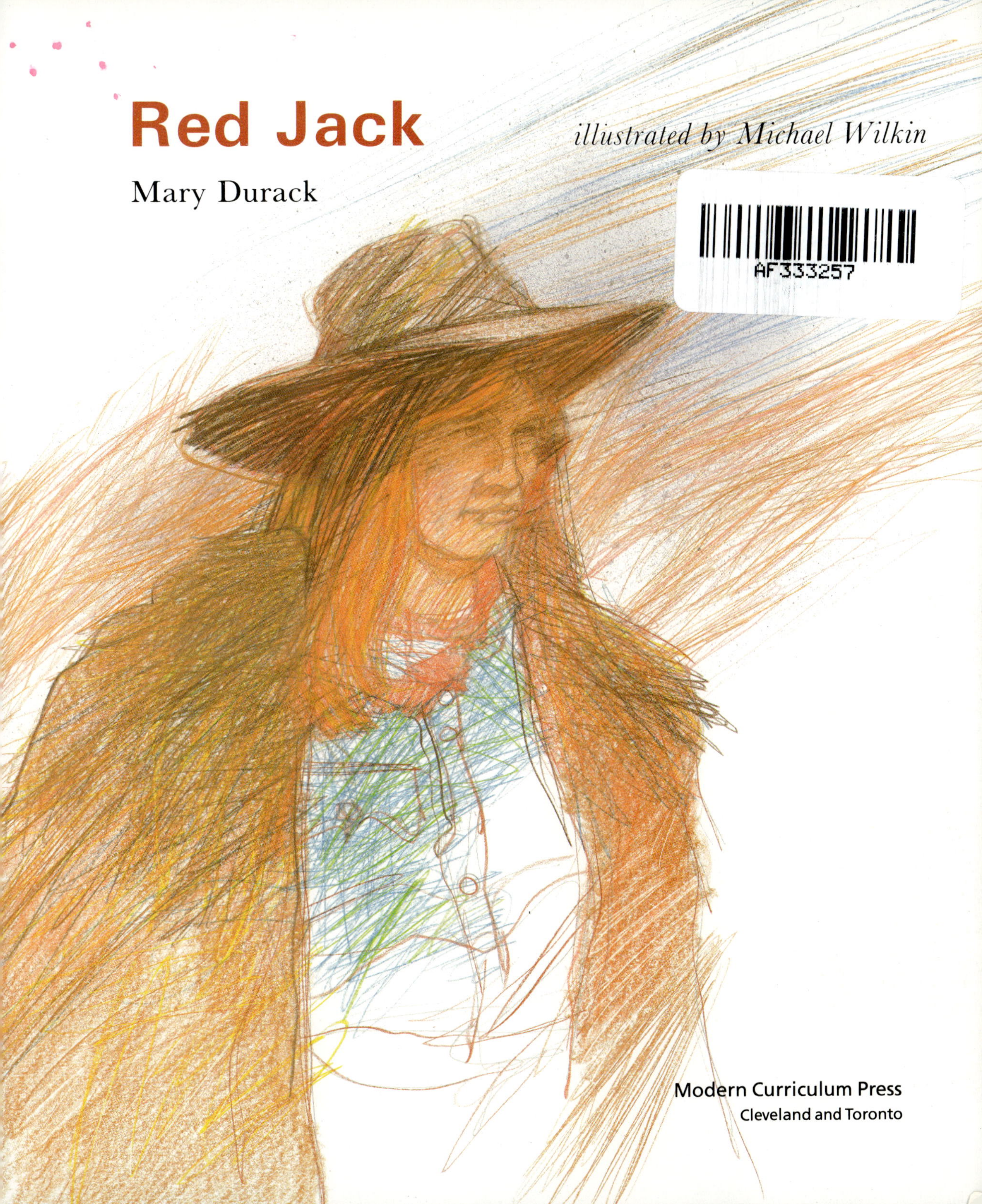

Modern Curriculum Press

Cleveland and Toronto

She rises clear to memory's eye
From mists of long ago,
Though we met but once, in '98 –
In the days of Cobb and Co.

'Twas driving into Hughenden
With mail and gold for load
That I saw Red Jack, the wanderer,
Come riding down the road.

Red Jack and Mephistopheles –
They knew them far and wide,
From Camooweal to Charters Towers,
The route they used to ride.

They knew them round the Selwyns where
The Leichhardt has its source,
Along the winding cattle ways –
A woman and a horse.

6

And strange the tales they told of them
Who ranged the dusty track:
The great black Mephistopheles
And the red-haired witch Red Jack.

She claimed no name but that, they said.
And owned no things but these:
Her saddle, swag and riding-kit
And Mephistopheles.

And often travellers such as I
Had seen, and thought it strange,
A woman working on the line
That crossed McKinlay Range.

Had seen her in the dreary wake
Of stock upon the plains,
Her brown hand quick upon the whip
And light upon the reins.

With milling cattle in the yard
Amid the dust-fouled air,
With rope and knife and branding iron –
A girl with glowing hair.

"Red Jack's as good as any man!"
  The settlers used to own;
And some bold spirits sought her hand,
  But Red Jack rode alone.

She rode alone, and wise men learned
To set her virtue high,
To weigh what skill she plied her whip
With the hardness of her eye.

I saw Red Jack in '98,
The first time and the last,
But her face, brown-gaunt, and her hair, red-bright,
Still haunt me from the past.

The coach drew in as she rode in sight;
We passed the time of day;
Then shuffled out the mail she sought
And watched her ride away.

And oh! her hair was living fire,
But her eyes were cold as stone:
Red Jack and Mephistopheles
Went all their ways alone.

24